Verus Jesuitarum Libellus
The True Book of the Jesuits

and the

Praxis Magica Fausti
Magickal Elements of Doctor John Faust

Verus Jesuitarum Libellus

The true Magical Work of the Jesuits; containing most powerful charges and conjurations for all evil spirits of whatever state - condition or office they are And a most powerful and approved conjuration of the Spirit Usiel; to which is added Cyprian's Invocation of Angels and his Conjuration of the Spirits Guarding Hidden Treasure - together with a form for their dismissal.

Paris 1508

Englished from the Latin by Herbert Irwin

- 1875-

The True Book of the Jesuits

"Somnia, terrores, magicos, miracula. Sagas nocturnos, lemures, portentaque thessala risu excipio"

- Horatius

1st Conjuration

I _N____ The most unworthy creature of our Lord J. C. and servant of God, beg, call, and exorcise thee, Spirits by Water ✠ air ✠ fire ✠ and by earth - and by all those which have life, being and moving therein - and by the most Holy name J. C. : Agios ✠ ischiros ✠ paracletus ✠ Alpha and Omega ✠ beginning and end ✠ God ✠ and Man ✠ Zebaoth ✠ Adonai ✠ Agla ✠ Tetragrammaton ✠ Abua ✠ Deus ✠ Eljon ✠ Jana ✠ Jehovah ✠ God ✠ Sachnaton ✠ arumna ✠ Messias ✠ Cherub ✠ Misol ✠ Ambriel ✠ Achteol ✠ Jachenas ✠ and by the power of God the Father ✠ and by the strength of God the Son ✠ and by the virtue of the Holy Spirit ✠ and by the words with which Solomon and Manasses exorcised the spirits and by the words which have power over thee ✠ That thou immediately, even as thou wert obedient to Isaac and to Abraham, render due obedience unto me, and appear before me, in a beautiful. mild and human form, and bring to me (out of the depths of the Seas) _N._____ millions of the best and true spanish gold without tumult or else I will condemn thy body and thy soul ✠ I command thee, abstaining from all harm and without noise, thunder, or tempest - without tenor and without trembling, to place thyself before me - beyond this circle, I command this to thee Spirit ✠ by the virtue of God the Father ✠ of God the Son ✠ and of God the Spirit ✠ and by the power with which all are created and made _____

✠ Let it be Done ✠

2nd Conjuration

I N_____ Servant of God ✠ command, call, and exorcise thee,
O Spirit! by the Holy apostles and disciples of God ✠ By the Holy
Evangelists ✠ By st Matthew ✠ By St Mark ✠ By St Luke ✠ By St
John ✠ and by the most holy men Shadrach ✠ Mesach ✠ and
Abednego ✠ and by all the holy Patriarchs ✠ Prophets ✠ and
Confessors ✠ Priests ✠ and Levites ✠ and by the chastity of all the
holy virgins ✠ and by the most holy and terrible words Aphriel Diefriel
✠ Zada ✠ Zadai ✠ Lamabo ✠ Lamogella ✠ Caratium ✠ Lamogellay
✠ Logim ✠ Lassim ✠ Lepa ✠ Adeo ✠ God ✠ aleu aboy ✠ aboy ✠
alonpion dhon ✠ Mibizime ✠ Mora ✠ Abda ✠ Zeud and by the most
holy Magi Caspai ✠ Milchisi ✠ and Balthusai ✠ and by that which
Solomon ✠ Manasseo ✠ Agrippa Cyprian Knew and exorcised the
spirits and by the ascension of Christ into the highest realms of peace
✠ That thou appearest before me in a beautiful affable, and human
form, and bring to me out of the depths of the waters N._____
without tumult, without hurt to me, without the noise of thunder and of
tempests, without terror, and without trembling, and place it before this
circle, and this I command to thee by the Most Holy Mary ✠ Mother of
God ✠ and by the principal merits of the Mother of God ✠

3rd Conjuration

I. _N_____ the servant of God call cite and command thee, Spirit, By all the holy angels and archangels ✚ by the holy Michael ✚ by the holy Gabriel ✚ By the holy Raphael ✚ by the holy Ariel ✚ by the holy Thrones ✚ Dominions ✚ Principalities ✚ Powers ✚ and Virtues ✚ by the Cherubim ✚ and by the Seraphim ✚ who incessantly proclaim by their voices Holy ✚ Holy ✚ Holy ✚ and by the most Holy word Noah Soter ✚ Emmanuel ✚ Adonai ✚ El ✚ Elly ✚ Elloy ✚ Braun ✚ Joseph ✚ Jona ✚ Calphia ✚ Calphas ✚ and by that word by which Solomon and Manasses, Agrippa and Cyprian, knew the spirits, and by that which the power to exorcise thee and as Jesus was obedient to his parents so be thou obedient unto me, and appear before me in a beautiful, affable, and human form, and bring to me out of the depths of the waters _____ without tumult, failing which I condemn thee both spiritually and materially, abstain from all evil towards me, and without noise, without thunder and without trembling and without fear, appear and place thyself before this circle, and this do I command thee by the power of God the Father God the Son and God the Holy Spirit ✚ I _N._____ do cite thee spirit of Iayariel to appear before me though aroram Lasunabula Sol Jesus Christus the victor by Schehostia Schelam Jehova Votmehasehla Schebevek adonay Proemischoea avit. By the wonderous power of the names agla Schaffort. And by the great spirit Jehova Podashocheia.

4th Conjuration

I *N.*_____ Servant of God, call command and exorcise thee, O Spirit! by the wisdom of Solomon ✛ by the obedience of Isaac ✛ by the blessing of the tribe of Abraham, by the piety of Jacob ✛ and of Noah ✛ who sinned not against God ✛ By the Serpent of Moses ✛ and by the twelve tribes of Israel ✛ and by the most holy words ✛ Abill ✛ Dellia ✛ Dellion ✛ Ensusellas ✛ Jazy ✛ Zatael ✛ Olam ✛ Dithaton ✛ Sathos ✛ Reckamaton ✛ Anab ✛ Illi ✛ Hogo ✛ Adathgiur ✛ Gueb ✛ Suna ✛ Amon ✛ Deuth ✛ alos ✛ Gaoth ✛ Egaoth ✛ Lilu ✛ and by the works with which Solomon, and Manasses, Agrippa and Cyprian Knew the spirits, and as God commanded His Most Holy Mother to St. John, when he was departing from this material world, so do I also commend myself to thee and do command thee immediately to appear before me in a beautiful, affable, and human form and bring to me out of the depths of the Sea _____ which if thou dost not I will condemn thee in body and soul, without hurt to me, without noise of thunder, nor tempest without terror and without trembling, and place it before me in this circle, This do I command thee by the most Holy Trinity ✛

5th Conjuration

I N._____ Servant of God , call, cite, and command thee O Spirit
_____ By the most holy incarnation of J. C. by the most Holy
Nativity ✝ Circumcision ✝ Flagellation ✝ coronation ✝ His bearing
of the Cross ✝ His ✝ Crucifixion ✝ his bitter passion, and death, and
Resurrection ✝ and his ascension ✝ by the sending of his holy
comforting Spirit ✝ and by the most terrible words of the God of Gods
Elhor ✝ Genio ✝ Jophiel ✝ Zophiel ✝ Camael ✝ Elemiach ✝ Richol
✝ Hoamiach ✝ Imaniach ✝ Namuel ✝ Damobiach ✝ and ✝ by those
words by which Solomon ✝ Manasses ✝ Agrippa ✝ and cyprian ✝
Knew the Spirits ✝ and by those words which have special power over
thee, as Jesus came into the world, even so come thou to me and appear
thou before me in a beautiful affable and human form, and bring to me
N. _____ out of the great abyss, which if thou does not I will
condemn thee to spiritual and material torments, abstaining from all
evil towards me, without noise either of thunder, or of tempest without
fear and without trembling, and place thyself before this circle, and I
command thee by the all powerful and Eternal God, that thou Spirit art
obedient unto me ✝

6th Conjuration

I *N.*_____ Servant of God, call, cite and exorcise thee Spirit! ✠
✠ By the bleeding and by the, sweating of J. C. by his Divine love and
Mercy, By his Providence ✠ omnipotence ✠ and immensity and by all
the virtues of J.C. and by all which he has suffered for the human race,
and by the seven words which he uttered when on the cross to his
Heavenly Father when he gave up his holy Spirit and by the most Holy
and terrible words, agios ✠ Tetragrammaton✠ Ischyros ✠ Athanatos
✠ Abua ✠Agla✠ Jod ✠ Jadoth ✠ Menoch ✠ Alpha and Omega ✠
Raphael ✠ Michael ✠ Uriel✠ Schmaradiel ✠ Zadia ✠ and by all by
which Solomon ✠ Manasses ✠ Agrippa ✠ and ✠ Cyprian ✠
assembled the Spirits ✠ and by which thou art summoned ✠ and even
as God shall come to judge the living and dead, so come thou to me and
appear before me in a beautiful affable, and human form, and bring to
me _____ out of the abyss of waters, which if thou dost not
I will curse thy body and soul, abstain from all harm, come without
noise of thunder or tempest, without terror and without trembling, and
place thyself before this circle, this do I command thee by the true
Living God

Fiat

7th Conjuration

I N._____ Servant of God do conjure, cite, and exorcise thee, O Spirit! by the five most holy wounds of J.C. by his flesh and blood, by his torments and passion, by his life and death and by the precious drops of blood which he has shed for the salvation and sanctification of the human race, by his anguish and distress, and by the most Holy and terrible words, Soter ✝ Choma ✝ Geno ✝ Jehovah ✝ Elohim ✝ Velaoch ✝ Divoch ✝ Alvoch ✝ Alrulam ✝ Stopiel ✝ Zophiel ✝ Jophiel ✝ fabriel ✝ Elopha ✝ Alesomas ✝ Difred Malach ✝ and ✝ by ✝ the words by which Solomon ✝ Manasses ✝ Agrippa ✝ and cyprian ✝ called together the Spirits, and even as J.C. sent from him his spirit, and delivered it up onto the hands of his heavenly Father, so do I command thee that thou appearest without delay, and comest before me, in a most beautiful affable and human form, and bring to me out of the Spiritual Abyss _____ without doing injury to me, without tumult - without thunder, without tempest, without fear, and without trembling and place before this circle, and this I command thee by the Deity and humanity of J.C.

Amen

To Discharge the Spirits

Now I command and charge thee Evil Spirit! that thou shalt bring to me immediately that which I commanded thee, and shalt depart from the circle, abstaining from all noise, terror, tumult, and ill savour, which if thou dost not I will punish thee both in body and in soul, abstaining from all evil to any creature or thing and depart immediately to the place which the justice of God hath set apart for you.

Depart from my sight thou cursed spirit, This I command thee in the name and virtue, potency and power, of the most Holy Trinity ✝ Father ✝ and Son ✝ and Holy Spirit ✝ Behold the Cross of Lord ✝ fly to the adverse parts ✝ The Lion of the tribe of Judah ✝ of the root of David conquers ✝ Allelujah ✝ Allelujah ✝ Allelujah ✝ Hasten now bring to me what I require, and depart from this circle, by the virtue of the name of our Lord J.C. and by virtue of his words which caused the Earth to tremble, In his name, and by his power I command thee, that thou dost immediately, and without delay withdraw thy accursed presence from my sight, by virtue of the words Messias ✝ Soter ✝ Emmanuel ✝ Zebaot ✝ Adonai ✝ Hagios ho ✝ Theos ✝ Ischyros ✝ athanatos ✝ Eleison ✝ hymas ✝ Tetragrammaton ✝ our Lord J.C. by that most Holy name I constrain ✝ thee, I force ✝ thee I compel ✝ thee and urge, and confine ✝ thee, to the place to which the justice of God hath sent thee, therefore recede immediately and continually, neither return hither again unless I do call thee, this I command by the uncreated Father ✝ by the uncreated Son ✝ by the uncreated Holy Spirit ✝ Behold the Cross of the Lord! ✝ By the sprinkling of the blood of J.C. ✝ by the virtue of the Holy Water ✝ by the virtue and power of the most High ✝ shalt disperse thee thou evil spirit ✝ The word is made flesh and dwells amongst us ✝ Amen

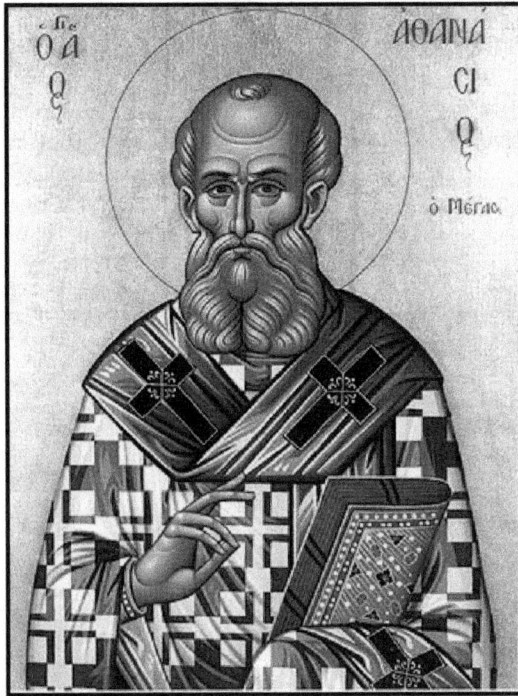

The Symbol of Athanasius, and "De profundis" are to be used:

De Profundis (Psalm 132)

A Song of Ascents. The Lord, remember unto David all his affliction; How he swore unto the Lord, and vowed unto the Mighty One of Jacob: 'Surely I will not come into the tent of my house, nor go up into the bed that is spread for me; I will not give sleep to mine eyes, nor slumber to mine eyelids; Until I find out a place for the Lord, a dwelling-place for the Mighty One of Jacob.' Lo, we heard of it as being in Ephrath; we found it in the field of the wood. Let us go into His dwelling-place; let us worship at His footstool. Arise, O the Lord, unto Thy resting-place; Thou, and the ark of Thy strength. Let Thy priests be clothed with righteousness; and let Thy saints shout for joy. For Thy servant David's sake turn not away the face of Thine anointed. the Lord swore unto David in truth; He will not turn back from it: 'Of the fruit of thy body will I set upon thy throne. If thy children keep My covenant and My testimony that I shall teach them, their children also for ever shall sit upon thy throne.' For the Lord hath chosen Zion; He hath desired it for His habitation: 'This is My resting-place for ever; here will I dwell; for I have desired it. I will abundantly bless her provision; I will give her needy bread in plenty. Her priests also will I clothe with salvation; and her saints shall shout aloud for joy. There will I make a horn to shoot up unto David, there have I ordered a lamp for Mine anointed. His enemies will I clothe with shame; but upon himself shall his crown shine.'

The Conjuration of Usiel

Hear Usiel, I N. _____ an unworthy Servant of God, conjure, require, conquer and call thee, O Spirit Usiel! Not by my power - but by the strength, virtue, and potency of God the Father and by the Redemption and Salvation of God the Son   and by the power and victory of God the Holy Spirit and by the strength and potency of the words Eli, Elé, Lama Assabtham Emmanuel Agios Tetragrammaton by Adonai Ejeh El Schadai Chije Ischyrion Agla Chab and Hoim Aron Alpha and Omega Ohoch Lauth Doffuaphi Lohuffo Rugo Dolah by the Father Lord by J.C. and by the Holy Spirit Allelujah by God of Abraham the God of Isaac the God of Jacob by the God who appeared to Moses his servant on Mount Sinia and who led the children of Israel out of the land of Egypt.   By this I conjure thee O spirit Usiel, be thou either on high or in the abyss   in water, or in fire, or in or in earth, I command thee Spirit Usiel immediately to appear before me in a proper human form, visibly to shew thyself and modestly to submit thyself, and readily to appear and bring to me out of the abyss of the Earth, or of the Sea, that which I desire, in all tranquility and patience, without tumult, without detriment to me, onto the bodies and souls of all created things,   without blinding, or dumbness, without falsity or fallacy, according to the manner in which I have called thee, without danger, without whispering, without thunder, without hail, without explosion, without puffing up, without trembling, and place yourself before this circle in that part which I appoint you

This I N_____ command thee Usiel by the holy passion of J.C. and by all the secret mysteries of J.C. and by all the Holy martyrs who gave up their bodies and their lives for Christ, and by all the words which have proceeded out of the mouth of the Creator of Heaven and of Earth against the Spirits of Evil, or I will again disturb, govern, and torture thee, when I have need of thee to perform my commands - Therefore be not disobedient, for I   N_____   conjure thee, command and compel thee, O Spirit Usiel! By the judgments of the Most High, and by the shining sea which is before the face of the Divinity, and by his Majesty, and by the angelical virtues of his omnipotence, and by that fire which is before the throne of God and by the domination of the sacred and Holy Trinity, by the song which is sung ever before the throne of by the holy angels "Gloria in Excelsis"! and by the most high wisdom of the Omnipotent and by the most terrible passing away of the Heavens and of the Earth, and by the most holy majesty of the names

17

Agla Noab Soter Emmanuel Adomatai Hurai Amaton Elle Eloi Vision Adon Madai Prog Joseph Jonas Calphia Calphas by the last and terrible day of Judgement by the power of Affei by the holy name Primeumaton which Moses used and Datan, Corah and Abyron were swallowed up into caverns and abysses of the Earth, by the power of the word Primeumaton and by the power which it exercises over the supercelestial and Celestial worlds, and by the strength and power of the sacred and holy names Chet Hetoi Agla Jad Rabonni Aglos Zachlor Septro Phanuel and Sion Onothion Seneon Olohe Lamech and by the potent name of J.C., and by the most High name, at which the whole world, and the Infernal Abyss trembles Dan Ana Agla Loth Bezer Phanum also by the spiritual efficacy of the words by which the Bread and Wine was changed into the body and blood of God "This is my body", "this is the command of the Lord thy God" the Merciful One Redeemer of the world have compassion on me and this do I N._____ order thee that thou Spirit Usiel shalt come immediately to this place, whether thou art in the Abyss of Hell, or the Earth, or in whatever parts thou mayest be, and shall appear, visibly and modestly in a human form before me, submitting thyself to me, and obediently bringing before this circle which I have marked that which I have commanded thee, This I N._____ order thee Spirit Usiel, not by my power, but by the strength virtue and potency of God the Father and by the binding of God the Son, and by the healing of God the Holy Spirit by the power of Tetragrammaton Agla Adonai Amen! Amen! Amen! Jesus! Sancta Maria! I command and order thee not to delay, but to do that which I have commanded thee! come! come! come! why dost thou delay? Hasten for I order thee, in the name of Adonai Shadai King of Kings El Ali Titeis Azia Hin Jen Chimosel Achadan vai va ej ha ejeh Eke hau hau hau va va va a el el a hy Requiel Atatriel Scholiel Hanel Hamaliel Phaiamech Oriph Machiduel Barbiel Zacheriel Orphiel Zamuel Rugo Hamaliel Ziriel come now by all the most powerful words Tetragrammaton adonai agla and by the wounds of J.C. by the prophets by the apostles and by all the saints who live with God in holiness by the power of Duisa and of Zebaoth Dujam Dujam Dujam.

The Angelical Citation of St. Cyprian

I call, cause, cite, and exorcise thee: O Almaziel Ariel Anathamia Ezebul Abiul Ezea Ahesin and Calizabin, by the most Holy Angels of God by all the dominations thrones powers and angelical principalities by all the beatitudes and ineffable delights of Heaven By the Angel which announced to the Shepherd the Incarnation and nativity of the Saviour, by the four and twenty elders who cry incessantly before the Divine throne. Holy Holy Holy is the Lord our God and by the Holy intercourse of the Angels who have the Knowledge of Jesus by the Cherubim and by the Seraphim and by all the archangels- by the infinity and omnipotency of God and by the creation of the world, that thou helpest me in this my need even as thou didst assist Lot and Abraham who were your hosts, as also Jacob and Moses Joshua and Samson and many others whom you have deigned to visit, come o ye angelic ones in beautiful form, full of dignity and brightness, and do all that which I have requested thee, in the name of the Triune Jehovah whose praises all spirits incessantly sing giving honour to the all Powerful who is thy Lord as he is mine.

Amen

When the Spirit Maketh Visible Apparition

Thou shalt say:

Adonai Zebaoth Adon Schadai Eljon Amanai Eljon Pneumoton Elji Alnoal Messias Ya Heynanan Tetragrammaton. Amen.

Then use the following Conjuration:

Adonai Zebaoth Adon Schadai Eljon Tetragrammaton Eloi Elohim Messias Ya Hagios ho Theos. Amen.

Then repeat the following Conjuration inwardly:

Alley Fortissian Fortissio Allinoson Ron.

The spirit is to be dismissed by the following:

Omysoma Epyn Segok Satany Degony Eparygon Galligonon Zagogen Ferstigon

A Conjuration compelling Obedience

I adjure, require, and command thee, Human Spirit who visiteth this place and hath in thy life hidden and buried thy treasure therein, that in this hour of the night, in the day of _____ in the month of _____ thou shall appear before me under the form of a fire, by the Ineffable name Jehovah, by the Ineffable and Incomprehensible Fiat, by the power of which all things are created, made known, and strengthened, I conjure, require, and adjure thee human Spirit, to appear visibly unto me beyond this circle, by the great goodness of God who hast created men in his own likeness, by the great power of his Justice, by virtue of which he has expelled the demons and hast enchained them within the Infernal Abyss, by the infinity of his mercy in sending his son to redeem us from the penalties of our sins, and by all the other Divine attributes and names, by the omnipotency of our savior J.C. by which he destroyed all the works of Hell and caused a blessing to fall upon the seed of the woman giving it power to crush the head of the serpent, that thou now answer me faithfully, rendering due obedience unto me, I conjure thee by the Ineffable name Tetragrammaton which is written on this role. that by the virtue of this most holy name thou shalt immediately render obedience unto me, answering me without deception, lying or equivocation, by virtue of the omnipotency of our savior who shall come to judge both the quick and dead, to judge both thee and me both the living and the dead.

Conjuration to be Used if the Spirit Refuseth Obedience to the Preceeding One.

I conjure thee human Spirit by the Ineffable name of God, written on this sheet which I dare not to pronounce and by my blood which was most sacred and excellently redeemed, and consecrated by the Lord of the Prophets J.C. by his most glorious Mother, by the insignia of his humility, by the great book of the judgements of God, by the terrible and last day of judgement , by all the angels, archangels and by all the host of Heaven that thou art obedient unto me, who art a Christian baptized in the holy waters of Jordan, and answer me faithfully without enigma, falsehood, or pretence, and on thy own part reveal to me truthfully and exactly what is the power that aids thee, this do I order thee by the most holy name of God, who has condemned thee to frequent and to guard this place in which thou hast buried thy treasure.

Amen! Amen! Amen!

Citation

Cohiziara Offina Alta Netera fuara Menuet
Cohiziara Offina Alta Netera fuara Menuet
Cohiziara Offina Alta Netera fuara Menuet

A Charge

Alim Jehoh Jehovah agla On Tetragrammaton.

The Dismissal of Cyrian

Now I conjure thee O Human Spirit! by the omnipotency, wisdom, and justice of God the Father of the Omnipotency of God the Son by the immensity of His Mercy and charity towards men by the omnipotency of the Holy Spirit, by his infinite wisdom, and inscrutable clemency By the Holy archangel Michael and all the host of Heaven, to abstain from lightnings from frightful and loud noises and tumult, without rain, and without thunder to be peaceable and quiet without danger or injury to our bodies or souls, I command thee to depart from this place, and to appear not again unless I summon thee May the peace of the Triune God, be with us now and preserve us from all danger O God be with us and have mercy upon us O God turn this Spirit N._____ to the path of righteousness and give us peace Glory be to the Father! And to the Son, and to the Holy Spirit

Amen

Finis April IX die Ionis
Anno Christi 1875

Praxis Magica Fausti

And the Magickal Elements of Doctor John Faust, Practitioner of Medicine. From the Original Manuscript in the Municipal Library of Weimar.

Passan Anno Adventionis Christi 1571.

Praxis Magica

Karuze ✭ Karoth ✭ Karathoi ✭ Kemelton ✭ Achatum Ella ✭ Dyestim ✠ Rim ✠ Warmat ✠ Ko ✠ Nemarram ✠ Palat ✠ Themat ✠ Amarrh ✠ Gyseton ✠ Ralapharos ✠ O Sachman ✠ Machey ✠ Gacles ✠ Bachat ✠ Gyrta ✠ Somon ✠ ✠ ✠ Now do I call thee ✠ ✠ ✠ Twsme ✠ Qaror ✠ amathema ✠ Jamhay ✠ Schea ✠ Stal ✠ Salmazan ✠ Pamphilos ✠ Aziel ✠ Alechemelor ✠ Raphael ✠ Salathiel ✠ Ve Sar ✠ Amathemach ✠ Heroe ✠ Somini ✠ By the loving Kindness of the Holy Incomprehensible and invisible God - which is displayed in all his works - for all things which he hath created are good and holy ✠ Barion Salmafan ✠ Raphael ✠ Neman ✠ Azan ✠ Raphael ✠ come thou I call thee vehemently ✠ O Spirit by the power and virtue of the letters which I have inscribed - do I command thee to give me a sign of thy arrival.

1 ☾ ☽ ✠

I command thee to be obedient unto me - and now is it the time of the great name Tetragrammaton and I command you to appear before me in a beautiful and pleasing form.

ΤΩΜΕΑΤΑΝΟΝ

Larabay ✛ Belion ✛ Sonor ✛ Soraman ✛ Bliar ✛
Sonor ✛ Arotan ✛ Niza ✛ Raphael ✛ Alazaman ✛
Eman ✛ Nazaman ✛ Tedoyl ✛ Teabicabal ✛ Ruos,
Acluaar ✛ Iambala ✛ Iochim ✛

AET ✛ Ω

Zebaman ✛ Sehemath ✛ Egibut ✛ Philomel ✛
Gazaman ✛ Delet ✛ Azatan ✛ Uriel ✛ Facal ✛
Alazamant ✛ Nisia ✛ By the most sacred and
holy mercy of God ✛ Zeyhomann ✛ Acluaas ✛ Niza ✛
Tachal ✛ Neciel ✛ Amatemach ✛ Her somini ✛ By this I
compel thee to appear unto me before this circle and to do
what I command thee -

Now do I conjure and command thee O Evil Spirit
by the powers of Heaven and by the words of life ✛ Maji,
Staeti, Sche, Agla, Naob, Sother, Emmanuel, Adonay ✛
Adomaty ✛ Auray ✛ Amaton, Elle ✛ Elloy ✛ Vision ✛ By
the great love of Jesus Christ and by his triumph over death
and hell and by the omnipotency of God - who is - who was
– and who ever shall be - by the word paymow – and
Mephistophilis and by the power of the words ✛ Tetragram
✛ Agla ✛ Adonay ✛ Amin ✛ Amin

J ✛ S ✛ M ✛

I command cite and conjure thee to come quickly
and without delay ✛ I call thee ✛ ✛ Requiet ✛ ✛

Hamaliel ✚ ✚ Hanel ✚ ✚ Atatiel ✚ ✚ Scholiel ✚ ✚ Phacamech Oriph ✚ ✚ Malchidaet ✚ ✚ Barbiel ✚ ✚ Zacheriel ✚ ✚ Oriphiel Zamuel ✚ ✚ Hamaliel ✚ ✚ Ziriel ✚ ✚ Rugs.

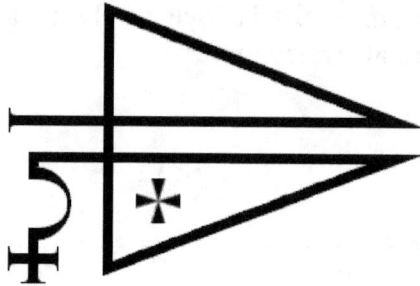

Come now I conjure thee by all the most powerful words Tetragrammaton Adoney Agla and by the wounds of J.C., by the Prophets, by the Apostles, and by all the saints who live in the holiness and love of God Come now by the mystic words ✚ Duisa ✚ Fortis ✚ Zebaoth. I do conjure thee to come ✚ Dujam ✚ Dujam ✚ Dujam

I conjure each and all of ye Spirits, by the seven archangels, Governors of the Planets, Ouphiel ✚ Zacheriel ✚ Samoel ✚ Michael ✚ Gabriel ✚ Raphael ✚ who are your Governors to do that which I command - In the name of the Triune God ✚ ✚ Amen.

Now I conjure thee to come from thy abode even from the farthest parts by these great and mighty names,

Tetragrammaton, Adonai, Agla, and to appear before me receiving and executing my demands truly and without falsehood I command thee O Spirit Rumoar, even by thy great sovereign Lucifer   I command thee in the name of God the Father ✝ of the Son ✝ and of the Holy Spirit ✝ and by the power of the name Jesus of Nazareth. Amen.